CONTENTS

THE SOURCES

Shakespeare was rather like a magpie when he wrote most of his plays. He was attracted by the brightest and best moments in other stories, he explored the most dramatic events in English history, took over love stories and developed existing characters. He was able to blend these elements from different sources into new plays, usually much more exciting and interesting than their originals. And Shakespeare wrote in a vivid, expressive way which made the audience feel the atmosphere of the places and events on stage. They laughed, cried and shared the feelings of the characters.

Shakespeare was a success. He and his friends ran one of the most popular theatre companies in London. Their performances of his plays and those of other writers packed in audiences of up to 3000 a time nearly every afternoon of the week.

It is encouraging to learn that Shakespeare's plays did not come to him out of nowhere in a flash of inspiration. At the beginning of the 1590s he began writing plays which were based on English history; a best-selling history book of the time, *Holinshed's Chronicles*, provided most of the information as well as thumbnail sketches of the kings and other people involved. A few years later he began working with existing romantic and comic

The love story of Pyramus and Thisbe portrayed in this engraving of 1538 was told by the Roman poet Ovid. Shakespeare uses it in *A Midsummer Night's Dream*.

stories. There was one book in particular which he knew well from his schooldays. It was called *Metamorphoses* by the Latin poet, Ovid. Ovid's stories were about transformations – changes which his characters found themselves going through. Sometimes these were frightening; for example, when humans changed into animals. Ovid's stories must have sunk deep into Shakespeare's imagination because his plays contain many echoes from them.

The story of *Pyramus and Thisbe* which is used in *A Midsummer Night's Dream* appears in Book 4 of *Metamorphoses*. It is striking how many details Shakespeare borrowed – even the crack in the wall through which the two lovers whisper. Pyramus blames the wall:

'Jealous wall, why do you stand in the way of lovers ?'

It is only a little step to make the Wall a character, as Shakespeare does in his play-within-a-play in *A Midsummer Night's Dream*, but it is a step which makes Shakespeare's version of the story much funnier.

The strangest transformation in *A Midsummer Night's Dream* is when **Bottom** is magically given a donkey's head and meets the Queen of the Fairies, who takes a fancy to him. Shakespeare based this part of his story on another Latin book well known to the Elizabethans, *The Golden Ass* by Apuleius. (Ass is another word for donkey.) He also used details from several earlier poems referring to **Oberon** and **Titania**, King and Queen of the Fairies. Robin Goodfellow, or **Puck** as he is usually called in the play, was a mischievous spirit from folklore.

Shakespeare's magic was in how he chose, mixed and developed elements from these different sources.

The sprite in this seventeenth-century illustration is Robin Goodfellow, also known as Puck.

EARLY PERFORMANCES

A PRIVATE FIRST PERFORMANCE?

There is a mystery about the first performance of *A Midsummer Night's Dream*. It seems that the play was written between 1593 and 1596 but we don't know for certain where it was first staged. Many scholars think that it was written for an aristocratic wedding and first performed as part of the celebrations. It is even possible that Queen Elizabeth was guest of honour.

Several flattering references to her are hidden in the play.

If this theory is true then, on this occasion, Shakespeare was writing for a small, educated audience. The grand house where the wedding party took place would have been richly decorated. We know that the Elizabethans loved feasts and dancing, pageants and spectacular shows of all kinds. The actors would have made the most of the occasion, creating effects which were not possible in the public theatres where they usually worked. They could have used candlelight, for example, and more delicate and complex music.

A PUBLIC SUCCESS

The script of *A Midsummer Night's Dream* was printed in London in 1600. The title page says that the play had been 'publicly' acted 'sundry times' – in other words, quite often. This suggests that, even if it had been originally written for a wedding party, *A Midsummer Night's Dream* was later staged in the public theatres to a large mixed audience and that it was popular. The actors must have thrown themselves into the varied moods of the play and made it a hit.

We know enough about the design of Elizabethan playhouses to

Title page of the first printed copy, 1600.

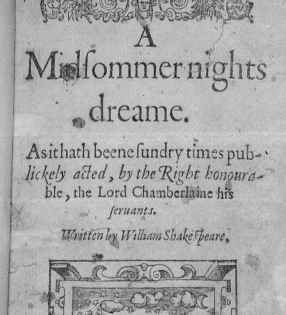

A
Midsommer nights
dreame.

As it hath beene sundry times pub-
lickely acted, by the Right honoura-
ble, the Lord Chamberlaine his
seruants.

Written by William Shakespeare.

Imprinted at London, for *Thomas Fisher*, and are to be soulde at his shoppe, at the Signe of the White Hart, in *Fleetestreete*. 1600.

imagine how some of the more tricky moments of action were achieved. There were two entrances to the stage through doors in the back wall and they led into dressing-room space. They enabled an exit, a quick change and an entrance through the other door – a perfect way of surprising the audience, for example, when **Bottom** suddenly has to appear with the ass-head. There was also an alcove covered by a curtain in the back wall, a natural place for the Queen of the Fairies' bower.

Music and dancing are an important element throughout this play and in Elizabethan times a band would have played live from the gallery above the stage along the back wall.

There are four women's parts in the play and, as usual, boys or young men were needed to play them. There were no actresses on the Elizabethan stage but boys scored a great success in the female roles. The two girls in the play, **Hermia** and **Helena**, are young and lively and have some marvellous comic moments, including a fullblooded row. We can imagine a couple of boys, perhaps about 12 years old without any sign of their voices breaking yet, having a lot of fun bringing these parts to life.

Titania would have been a harder challenge for a young male actor. She speaks some of the most highly descriptive language in the play and goes through a range of very strong emotions. She has to be convincing as a 'fairy', part of the supernatural world, yet in her feelings she is very human.

The Elizabethans loved shows and celebrations: this is a Water Show organized in Hampshire in 1591 to entertain Queen Elizabeth.

The Characters

The characters fall into three groups: those associated with Duke Theseus and his court; the workmen of Athens; the fairies in the wood. The story of the play brings people from each of these groups into contact with each other with comic, romantic and disturbing results.

Theseus Duke of Athens, a man of authority. He has just returned triumphant from war against the Amazons.

Hippolyta Queen of the Amazons, a tribe of warlike women. She was defeated in battle by Theseus and brought back to Athens where he intends to marry her. She doesn't seem keen on the idea – he was her enemy not long before!

A miniature painting by Nicholas Hilliard, 1590. The young nobleman is dressed very richly, perhaps for Court or a wedding. The actors playing Lysander and Demetrius would have been dressed rather like this.

Lysander A young nobleman in love with Hermia.

Demetrius Another young nobleman in love with Hermia. He used to love Helena.

Hermia A young lady who loves Lysander. She has a strict father. She is rather short.

Helena A young lady who loves Demetrius. She is Hermia's best friend and they went to school together. She is tall.

Egeus Hermia's father. He wants her to marry Demetrius even though she loves Lysander. He has a temper and is even prepared to see her in a nunnery or killed if she disobeys him.

Philostrate In charge of entertainment at Theseus's Court. He has his own ideas about who is suitable to be presented at Court. He is a bit of a snob.

Oberon King of the Fairies. He is a master of magic power and uses it to get his own way.

Titania Queen of the Fairies. She is a creature of the wood and in close harmony with the natural world. She and Oberon have had a row and are avoiding each other at the beginning of the play.

Puck or **Robin Goodfellow** Oberon's chief attendant. He is well known for practical jokes and general mischief.

Peaseblossom, **Cobweb**, **Moth**, **Mustardseed** Fairies in Titania's service.

Peter Quince A carpenter and the organizer of the rehearsals for *Pyramus and Thisbe*. He is the man with the difficult task of getting a decent performance out of his actors. He gives out the parts and directs the rehearsals. When they eventually perform at Court he gives a Prologue which introduces their play to the Duke.

Nick Bottom A weaver who plays **Pyramus**. He is the star actor, and knows it! He is magically changed by Puck who gives him an ass-head. He then finds that the Queen of the Fairies has taken a fancy to him.

Francis Flute A bellows-mender. He is still quite young – almost a boy – but boasts that he has a beard coming so couldn't possibly play a woman's part. Peter Quince insists, however, that he plays **Thisbe**, the heroine of the story.

Tom Snout A tinker who plays **Wall** in the play.

Snug A joiner who plays **Lion**. He says that he is slow at learning lines and is relieved that he only has to roar.

Robin Starveling A tailor who plays **Moonshine** in the play.

WHAT HAPPENS

'The course of true love never did run smooth'

Theseus, Duke of Athens, has just returned from fighting against the warlike Amazons. He has brought back their Queen, **Hippolyta**, whom he wishes to marry.

Egeus is determined that his daughter, **Hermia**, will marry the young man of his choice, **Demetrius**. Hermia is in love with **Lysander**. Egeus brings all three young people to see the Duke and begs for his support in forcing them to accept his wishes. Lysander argues that he is just as suitable a husband as Demetrius, with the advantage of being loved by Hermia. What's more, he reminds everyone that Demetrius used to be in love with **Helena** who is now broken-hearted because he has switched his attention to Hermia.

Egeus appeals to an ancient law of Athens which says that a father can arrange his daughter's marriage entirely as he wishes. Theseus agrees that the law does allow this and points out to Hermia the choices she has: to agree to marry Demetrius as her father wants or to enter a convent as a nun or to die. He gives her a few days in which to make up her mind.

Lysander and Hermia try to console one another and Lysander explains his plan. They will run away in the middle of the night and set off for his aunt's house some distance from Athens. He expects to find a welcome there, and the chance to marry. And he hasn't forgotten that his aunt is rich!

Helena, Hermia's best friend, appears and they tell her what they have decided to do.

Left alone, Helena pours out her feelings. She is miserable because Demetrius ignores her now and she is envious of the love between Hermia and Lysander. She decides to tell Demetrius what they are going to do. She thinks that he will follow them so as not to lose Hermia and she will follow him. Perhaps he might even be grateful to her.

QUINCE, BOTTOM AND COMPANY

A group of workmen gathered together by **Peter Quince** are going to rehearse a play to present to the Duke as part of his wedding celebrations. It will be the tragic love story of **Pyramus and Thisbe**. Quince has some trouble in keeping **Nick Bottom** in order – he wants to play all the best parts.

FAIRYLAND

Oberon and **Titania**, King and Queen of the Fairies, have fallen out. Whenever they meet, a furious argument starts. They accuse each other of being unfaithful (in fact, of Oberon loving Hippolyta and of Titania loving Theseus). They quarrel over a little Indian boy who is one of Titania's followers and whom Oberon wants as his page. Titania won't give him up because she was fond of his mother who died in childbirth. She points out to Oberon that their quarrel is disturbing the natural cycle of the seasons and that this causes suffering to human life as harvests fail and the weather is topsy turvy. He doesn't care.

'Ill-met by moonlight, proud Titania.' Paul Scofield as Oberon and Susan Fleetwood as Titania in Bill Bryden's 1982 production for the National Theatre.

Oberon plots with **Puck**, his chief fairy attendant, to take revenge on Titania. Puck is to find a flower whose juice has magical properties. Oberon will use it to make Titania fall madly in love with the next living thing she happens to see. He hopes it will be something vile.

Confusion in the Wood

Hermia and Lysander are tired and have lost their way in the wood. They lie down to sleep.

Demetrius has followed them but is infuriated by Helena following him. He threatens violence if she doesn't go away: she is thoroughly miserable.

Puck has brought the love-juice to Oberon. He squeezes some of it into Titania's eyes as she sleeps. Oberon has overheard Demetrius and Helena. He pities Helena and wants to make Demetrius love her, so he tells Puck to use the love-juice on him. He will recognize Demetrius by his Athenian style of dress. Puck squeezes the juice on to the eyes of the first Athenian man he finds but it is Lysander, the wrong man. Lysander wakes, sees Helena and immediately declares undying love. Helena is annoyed because she thinks he is teasing her.

Hermia wakes after a frightening dream and is worried to find that Lysander is nowhere in sight.

Rehearsal in the Wood

Peter Quince has called together his company of actors to rehearse in the wood at night away from prying eyes. All of them, except Bottom, are anxious about the parts they have to learn and the thought of appearing in front of the Duke but Quince manages to get a rehearsal of sorts going. Puck, an invisible onlooker, decides to have some fun. When Bottom exits behind a tree Puck transforms him by giving him an ass-head. Bottom's appearance terrifies his friends, who run away.

Ill-matched Couples

To keep up his spirits Bottom starts singing and wakes up Titania. Since Bottom is the first living thing she sees she immediately falls in love with him. Her fairies attend him and he is escorted off to her bower. Puck reports this success to Oberon, who is delighted.

They see Demetrius followed by Hermia. She believes that he must have killed Lysander out of jealousy. Demetrius is still declaring love to Hermia so Oberon realizes that Puck has made a mistake. He is sent off to find Helena, and Oberon uses the love-juice on Demetrius's eyes while he is asleep. Puck brings in Helena with Lysander still pursuing her; she is now at her wits' end. The noise they make wakes Demetrius who sees Helena and, of course, expresses passionate love too. Helena flips – this is too much, she doesn't deserve to be mocked so cruelly.

Bottom and Flute rehearsing *Pyramus and Thisbe*, in the woods. Desmond Barritt as Bottom and Daniel Evans as Flute in Noble's 1994 RSC production.

Chaos is really let loose when Hermia arrives on the scene. At first Hermia also believes that Lysander is teasing her friend and she asks him not to be unkind. Lysander answers her so roughly that she realizes he means it: he now loves Helena and not her. Hermia flips too – into furious anger against Helena whom she accuses of bewitching Lysander and stealing him from her. There follows one of the most famous and comic rows in English theatre.

Oberon and Puck have had a good laugh at the humans' expense.

CONFUSION UNTANGLED

Oberon takes pity on Titania's infatuation with Bottom and lifts the magic from her. She is glad to leave the strange sleeping creature, a human with an animal head. She and Oberon make up their quarrel. (Oberon had taken the little Indian boy whilst she was occupied with Bottom.)

Puck lifts the ass-head off Bottom.

The four lovers have been arranged into two pairs at last and then put to sleep by Puck. They are woken by the sound of Theseus's hunting horns to find themselves in early daylight, on the edge of the wood not lost in it, surrounded by people they recognize. Life seems almost back to normal and they doubt their strange memories of the past night and think they must have been dreaming. Theseus rules that they

will be married at the same time as he and Hippolyta: Lysander to Hermia and Demetrius to Helena.

Bottom wakes alone in the wood. He thinks he has been dreaming.

Back in Athens, Quince and the others are full of gloom. Bottom has been bewitched and has disappeared so their performance cannot take place. They are overjoyed when Bottom suddenly appears and the show can go on.

CELEBRATIONS AT COURT

The play of *Pyramus and Thisbe* is chosen by Theseus as the entertainment to be presented at Court after the wedding.

The actors, including poor Peter Quince, are terrified – all except Bottom who has a wonderful time over-acting. It's supposed to be a tragic love story but it becomes a farce.

There are some critical comments during the performance, especially from the young lovers who are in high spirits. But at the end the Duke seems to have enjoyed it and thanks the actors. Bottom leads the company in a lively dance, the Bergomask. He, Quince and the others have fulfilled their ambition – they have given a performance at Court.

MIDNIGHT

The newly married couples go to bed and, as midnight strikes, the fairies arrive in the palace. They bless the house and weave a spell to bring happiness to the marriages.

Puck has the last word in the form of an Epilogue to the audience. He says that they have seen nothing more real than a dream, begs their forgiveness if anything has caused offence and asks for their 'hands' – applause usually follows !

'Gentles, perchance you wonder at this show...' Bottom and his friends perform the play of *Pyramus and Thisbe* to the Duke and his Court. Howard Crossley as Wall with Pyramus and Thisbe in Noble's production.

THEMES IN THE DREAM

A *Midsummer Night's Dream* is a wonderful, complicated story full of comedy and surprises for the audience. Shakespeare has created characters which we recognize as true to life in all its complexity and confusion. The play is also much more. It creates a world which mirrors our inner world of dreams, longings and fears: sometimes frightening and dangerous, sometimes beautiful. It is a world in which magic happens and prompts us to ask what magic really is. Might it be the power of our imagination and our inner desires? This is one of the questions running through the play.

The questions which a play presents and the ideas which it develops are often called its themes. The themes of *A Midsummer Night's Dream* could be summed up as mischief, magic, marriage and they are intertwined.

When directors, designers and actors approach a play they often explore its themes from many different points-of-view. Eventually decisions are made about how their understanding of

Titania asleep with Bottom, while Puck and Oberon perform their mischief and magic. Open air performance in Regents Park, 1991.

the themes of the play will be expressed in the set design, the use of light and colour, the style of music and in the performances themselves.

The themes of a play like *Julius Caesar* are fairly clear: they are about political ideas and the private emotions of friendship, loyalty and love. *A Midsummer Night's Dream* is a different sort of play. Its themes strike the audience in a richly imaginative way. It is a play which both tells us a story and gives us a new experience: our own inner dreamworld is touched.

MISCHIEF AND MAGIC

One of the most striking characters in the play is **Puck** who is out for all the fun he can get. He enjoys creating chaos, particularly amongst humans, and says,

'Lord, what fools these mortals be!'

The mischief-making is not simply fun. Puck is the fixer for **Oberon** who is a complex character. He shows the common human feelings of jealousy and spite. **Titania** won't give him the boy he wants to join his followers and a fairyland version of tug-of-love begins. Oberon is determined to get what he wants and to punish Titania. He enjoys using his magic to make her fall in love with the 'next vile thing' she sees. In fact this is **Bottom** with the ass-head.

This turn of events is both comic and grotesque, perhaps even cruel. What goes on when they meet is extraordinary: Bottom is surrounded by flowers and music, he is treated like a king with tiny servants to bring him whatever he desires, he is entertained by a princess or spirit. Everything is strange, beautiful and aimed at pleasure. Yet the magic has a disturbing edge for the audience: even though Bottom has become an absurd thing – part man, part animal – he is, in fact, being seduced. Titania takes him off to bed.

When Oberon restores Titania to her 'normal' state he has got what he wanted – the little Indian boy – but Titania has been tricked, and so has Bottom who is left with nothing but a memory. Oberon's power is impressive, but dangerous.

MAGIC AND THE WOOD

The fairy world with its magic is connected with the natural world and night-time. Titania, in particular, is a creature of the wood. She has a 'bower' – a hidden place beneath the trees – and her fairies are named after plants and other natural things. They are realistic about the dangers of the natural world, such as snakes, but they 'charm' them away. The charm which Titania's fairies cast over the wood is associated with beauty and pleasure – they sing a lullaby to rock her to sleep and to ward off danger. The female fairies are close to nature and work in harmony with it.

It is a very attractive idea but, as usual with this play, just as we think that we can take a reassuring view of things our security is disturbed. Titania's fairies fail to keep her out of danger. Their lullaby is useless against her main enemy, Oberon. He takes advantage of her sleep to drop the love-juice on her eyes.

The difference between Oberon and Titania is made clear when she expresses her concern that their quarrel has disturbed the balance of the seasons. She wants them to create harmony not disruption.

The fairy kingdom is closely connected to the natural world of the wood. Out of this mix comes a kind of magic which causes a state of confusion that can be comic, tender, disturbing or beautiful. It is something to be both desired and feared.

MARRIAGE

At the end of the play three couples marry and the King and Queen of the Fairies are reunited. At first sight this might seem like a simple happy ending: true love has worked out in the end and led to marriage. But a closer look at the play raises several questions about these relationships. Love and marriage are not, after all, easy to achieve.

Theseus and **Hippolyta** are the human equivalents of the King and Queen of the Fairies but, in contrast, they have no freedom to follow their own desires.

At the opening of the play we see them waiting for their wedding. Theseus is impatient for the day to come, Hippolyta says very little and appears to be reluctant. They seem closer during the scene in the wood in the early morning when they are both enjoying the hunt. During the final scenes at Court their conversation flows more freely but there is never any sense of real intimacy between them.

For the four young people,

'The course of true love never did run smooth'.

At first their story is about the pains of infatuation. At the end it seems they may have learnt more about themselves and that perhaps now they are ready for love. But it is not certain.

When the fairies come at midnight to bless the house and the marriages they spread 'glimmering light' and 'field dew' gifts from their world of magic and nature. These enrich the marriages which have just begun.

Wealthy Elizabethans enjoyed arranging private entertainment in their houses for guests. This is a section from a painting of 1596, celebrating the life of Sir Henry Unton. It shows the interior of his house with a masque (musical entertainment) taking place. It is an occasion very like that which Philostrate arranges for Theseus, Hippolyta and their guests after their wedding.

Directors' Perspectives

The Roles of the Director and Designer

A Midsummer Night's Dream has been frequently performed this century. It fascinates directors and designers, and is a favourite with audiences.

The director of a production guides the development of all the actors' performances through the rehearsal process. The director has overall responsibility for the interpretation of the play. This involves a detailed look at the text of the play (the words). In A Midsummer Night's Dream one fundamental decision to be made is how to portray the **fairies** and the wood. There are also choices to be explored with the actors about their characters. For example, how far is **Oberon** cruel in his treatment of **Titania**? Is **Bottom** mainly a figure of fun or someone more complex and sympathetic?

In making these decisions the director has to work closely with the designer who creates the visual aspects of the production. S\he will make basic decisions about the shape and layout of the stage, fixing different points for exits and entrances, and possibly creating platforms and different levels for the actors to use.

One of the challenges for any designer of this play is to create an acting space which is flexible enough to suit all three strands:

- **Theseus's** Court
- the rehearsals of **Quince** and his friends
- the world of the fairies and the wood.

Max Reinhardt

Max Reinhardt was a German director who directed 22 of Shakespeare's plays. He tackled The Dream in twelve separate productions. The first was in Berlin in 1905 and the final one was his famous Hollywood film of 1935. Reinhardt was fascinated by the play in which he constantly found new ideas to explore.

His earliest production created a forest of real tree trunks and branches with a carpet of moss on the stage. A later production in 1910, at the large Deutsches Theater in Berlin, continued with a magnificently real wood but also used the latest technical theatre devices. The Deutsches Theater had a huge revolving stage, a structure like a giant turntable with different scenes set up on it in advance. A great advantage of the revolving stage for *The Dream* was the speed with which the scene could be changed. Whilst the audience saw Theseus in his Court at the beginning of the play the wood was ready to be put in place with one turn of the stage.

Reinhardt also used a 'cyclorama' and an electric wind machine to create spectacular effects. A cyclorama is a curving back wall or curtain, usually white, on which special lighting effects can be created. Thousands of light bulbs were fitted behind the cyclorama to create a starry sky. Reinhardt used the new theatre technology to create his own form of magic.

Max Reinhardt's production in Berlin in 1905 had Puck leading the lovers through a wood of real trees.

BEYOND REALISM

In London in 1900 there was a production by Henry Beerbohm Tree which featured real rabbits nibbling real grass. It was a great success but soon directors and designers developed other ideas.

The influential director and scholar of Shakespeare, Harley Granville Barker, believed that the text of the play was of supreme importance. He didn't want the audience looking at the set rather than listening to the actors so the designs he used were less detailed and did not attempt to look like real places.

The final dance of the fairies in Harley Granville Barker's production in 1914.

He worked with the designer Norman Wilkinson and they gave a completely new look to the **fairies**. Victorian productions had usually gone for pretty stage pictures with fairies dressed in droopy white dresses. Wilkinson covered them in gold make-up and dressed them in costumes which looked rather Indian – rich jewelled turbans and slim skirts in colours like scarlet and mauve.

He was most original of all in the way he created the wood. A curtain made of very fine fabric was drawn across the stage so that it hung in loose folds. It was painted in shades of gold with a dappled, abstract pattern which suggested trees and leaves. He also experimented with the lighting and flooded the stage with bright white light from lamps

attached to the front of the dress circle of the theatre.

MODERN PRODUCTIONS

Sir Peter Hall has directed *The Dream* three times on stage and once on film. He was also the first director of Benjamin Britten's opera of the play. Peter Hall and his designers have always located the play within the set of an Elizabethan country house and its surroundings. His aim has been

'to take The Dream *back to its beginnings, perhaps for a wedding in a country house.'*

Shakespeare set his story in ancient Athens yet all the descriptions of the wood are like the Warwickshire countryside where he grew up. **Bottom**, **Quince** and the others are the kind of men Shakespeare would have known in Stratford where his father was a glove-maker. Peter Hall's productions have always emphasized the Englishness of the

atmosphere and setting of *The Dream.*

The transformation of the stage setting from Theseus's house to the wood has been achieved in various ingenious ways. In the set of Peter Hall's 1959 production the floor of an Elizabethan manor house was covered with rushes and there was an upper minstrels' gallery. Gauze, painted with the front view of the house, was hung at gallery level. A gauze is a very fine sheet of netting which, when painted looks solid when lit from the front but disappears completely when lit from behind. Changing the direction of lighting on the gauze had the effect of making it disappear. So, in a second, the audience saw not the house but trees and bushes in a soft, misty light receding to the back of the stage. The two worlds; Theseus's court and the fairies' wood were both present.

Peter Hall's production in 1959 was played on a set of an Elizabethan Manor House.

New Dreams

When the director, Peter Brook, began rehearsing *The Dream* at Stratford in 1970 he was concerned about presenting this play about magic and fairies to an audience which was unlikely to believe in either. He saw the task of making the magical world of the fairies believable to a twentieth-century audience as crucial to the success of the play. He wrote:

'(It) is such a difficult and strong and clear starting point that everything else stems from that.'

He believed *The Dream* was a 'celebration'.

... a play by an adult writing very clearly and consciously for adults a play about fairies'

And he saw it as a series of transformations or changes.

'Theatre' as a Theme of the Play

Linked to the theme of transformation is the idea of theatre itself.

Actors performing in a play change into different characters, the stage becomes a different place, all kinds of effects surprise the audience.

The theatre is, itself, a kind of magic.

Brook therefore wove many obvious elements of the theatre into the way the actors performed. They practised and perfected some breath-taking performance skills. **Puck** stilt-walked; the **fairies** became expert trapeze artists; **Oberon** and Puck learnt how to juggle and spin plates.

Such acrobatic feats were very enjoyable to watch. It was also a pleasure to see the logic of how they were used. The flower which contains the love-juice was a plate spinning on a stick passed expertly from Puck to Oberon while they were both on trapezes. This was their cleverest trick used for the most powerful magic ingredient, the flower.

Brook felt that he had found a fresh way of presenting *The Dream*.

Design of the Set

Peter Brook and the designer, Sally Jacobs, wanted to keep the scope of the play as wide as possible so were not interested in any kind of fixed or realistic setting. They decided on a white box: three white walls and a gallery around the top from which actors could watch the play below. This made a neutral setting – there was no wood, no country house.

The audience was not given a pretty picture which helped to tell the story. Brook and Jacobs wanted to stimulate their audience into responding to the inner meanings of the play.

A particularly effective example of this is how Sally Jacobs created an equivalent to the wood. There were no real trees, but suspended from fishing rods in the gallery were long coils of wire. These became the obstacles through which the lovers had to fight their way. The fairies controlled the fishing rods above the stage and sent the coils of wire swinging dangerously over the stage even, at one point, chasing **Hermia** as she tried to escape through the auditorium. This original way of presenting the fairies' magic showed that they were in control, mischievously creating difficulties for the humans.

Peter Brook's production in 1970 set the play in a plain white box.

ACTORS' PERSPECTIVES

PLAYING THE COMEDY

Directors this century have enjoyed creating new settings and meanings for *The Dream*. Actors have a different challenge. They must bring to life words which were written 400 years ago. They must recreate the comic situations and make them funny for a twentieth-century audience.

Cheek By Jowl theatre company created a very strong situation for the comic characters in its modern-dress production in 1985. It presented **Quince**, **Bottom** and the others as typical members of an amateur dramatic society. It was a parody – a send-up – which used stock types of personalities. The audience laughed in recognition of the types of people they saw on stage. There was the terribly serious actor who withdrew into a corner to meditate before rehearsal, and an over-the-top enthusiastic Bottom in a dog collar. This was the Reverend Nick Bottom, the local vicar who fancied himself as an actor. The actor Colin Wakefield succeeded in making him both very funny and likeable.

In Peter Brook's production (see pages 24–25) the same group of characters were played, not as instantly recognizable types from everyday life but as fully rounded people. The comedy they achieved was gentle. The audience didn't laugh at *them* but rather at the common anxieties and little weaknesses which they showed.

Colin Wakefield as the Reverend Nick Bottom in Cheek by Jowl's production in 1985.

IMPROVISATION AND THE UNEXPECTED

The actor David Waller, who played Bottom in Brook's production has talked about the use of improvisation and games in rehearsal. He used it to explore what it would be like to be 'transformed', as Bottom is, into an ass, or to see your friend so shockingly changed, as the others do. Improvisation is an exercise used to dig deep into a situation or feeling in a play. The actors don't use the words in the play but freely create the scene with their own words and actions. David Waller wrote:

'We did an enormous number of quite extraordinary improvisations on the theme of transformed nightmares in magic woods . . . trying to think what would actually happen . . .'

The result of this was that the audience shared the other actors' shock and watched in fascination as Bottom,

visually changed only by a black nose and large donkey's ears sticking through his cap, gradually acted more and more as an animal. He pawed the ground with his foot, all his movements changed and finally, he let out a terrifyingly convincing ee-oohh, the bray of a donkey. He continued to let out this sound at moments throughout his speech, which was both comic and unnerving.

In 1989 the director John Caird achieved a box office success with his exuberant production. The **fairies** wore tattered ballet tutus with Doc Martens, and at odd moments would settle down to read *The Beano*. The actor, Richard McCabe, played **Puck** as a cult hero who signed autographs for the fairies, who were his fans. Rather than singing **Titania** to sleep the fairies had a disco. The comedy in these performances was achieved by wit and the unexpected.

Titania's (Clare Higgins') bower was an old brass bedstead and her fairies read *The Beano* in John Caird's production in 1989.

PLAYING THE FAIRIES

In the nineteenth century the parts of Puck and **Oberon** were usually played by young actresses. Ellen Terry, who went on to be the greatest Shakespearean actress of her generation, played Puck at the age of eight. Her first entrance was seated on a mushroom through a trap door. Other female Pucks and Oberons were elegant to look at but had little personality.

Actors in the twentieth century have reclaimed the parts of Oberon and Puck. They usually play them as strong, complex, *male* characters.

The choices to be made about how to play Puck are part of the exploration of the whole fairy kingdom. Peter Hall's three productions (see page 23) presented the fairies as more earthy and natural than the humans, and Puck was closest of all to the animal world. When Ian Holm played the role he panted eagerly like a dog and sniffed the air on scenting the approach of humans. He was an interesting contrast to Oberon, played by Ian Richardson with great elegance of voice and movement. Puck was of the earth but this Oberon was aristocratic, the obvious master of the fairy kingdom and all its powers.

Titania and her fairies had a different quality: the capacity to charm, to weave spells. Titania, played by Judi Dench, had a natural beauty. In a film version of the production she played her almost naked, very much a creature of the

Ellen Terry as Puck.

wood. Judi Dench also gave the character of Titania a sense of humour and fun. She was delighted and almost laughing at herself as she realized how much she had fallen for Bottom, for instance.

Peter Brook's famous production (see pages 24–25) presented the fairies very much as a group. There were only four of them and they were physically quite hefty. They were the unseen spirits who caused mischief and confusion at every opportunity. They made the wood an unsettling place for the four lovers, a place full of strange noises where things mysteriously moved and disappeared. They were a menacing reminder of the uncertainty of life.

THESEUS/OBERON, HIPPOLYTA/TITANIA

Several recent productions have had one actor playing both Theseus and Oberon and one actress to play Hippolyta and Titania. This is called doubling.

Peter Brook explained:

'The couples are so closely related that we felt that Oberon and Titania could easily be sitting inside the minds of Theseus and Hippolyta.'

The fairies in the wood have more freedom, more fun and pleasure than people do in ordinary life. Oberon and Titania are like the other, freer sides of Theseus and Hippolyta, the sides which are expressed in fantasies and dreams. John Carlisle played Theseus\ Oberon in 1989. He wore large pointed ears and little fairy wings as Oberon and combined flowing, dramatic speaking of the verse with a tremendous sense of fun. His Theseus, in contrast, was formal and restrained.

In Peter Hall's 1969 film the fairies were 'earthy, their flesh green-grey like moss and soil'. Here Titania (Judi Dench) is with her fairies.

A Fairy Story For Adults

T he theatrical history of *A Midsummer Night's Dream* reflects the changing tastes and interests of audiences. Each new generation of actors has re-created the play for its own time and this great range of interpretations shows the play's richness.

Oberon, Puck and Titania – three tough characters who bewildered the humans, in Peter Brook's production. "Lord what fools these mortals be!"

Many children are taken to see *The Dream* as their first Shakespeare play. Its comedy and the story of the fairies and the young lovers are entertaining for even quite young children.

It is a mistake, however, to think of *The Dream* as just for the young, charming but simple. As with traditional fairy stories there are elements in the play which can disturb us. We can enjoy the let's pretend aspect of the theatre on one level and be disturbed by a strange or twisted view of reality on another. A satisfying production of the play will both entertain and unsettle us. It will make us think.

Oberon's pleasure in tricking **Titania** with the love-juice is sometimes shown as violent and sexual. All the women in the play suffer to some extent from dominating, cruel men. The confusion of the lovers is also more than simply comic, their whole perception of life and of their own feelings is turned upside down. As members of the audience we don't watch a performance in a detached way; our minds, imaginations and feelings are affected. The mood in which the different strands of the story come together at the end is the mood in which we will go home; it's what we will remember.

A fundamental question for any director, therefore, is how far the ending of the play creates harmony. Can the audience go home enjoying a sense of peace and security?

The special occasion of a royal wedding brings together the Duke and some of his least important subjects, a group of workmen. This seems, at first, a satisfying event but the response which **Quince** and his actors earn for their performance is disappointing. The lovers laugh at their efforts, so the gulf between the Court and working men is not properly bridged. Actors have a real choice here about *how* they say the lines. Hippolyta's line, 'This is the silliest stuff that ever I heard', can be said in a sneering or an affectionate way, for instance.

Peter Hall (see page 23) is one contemporary director who chose to express a final sense of harmony between the different elements in the play. **Theseus** sincerely thanked the players and acknowledged the goodhearted loyalty behind the performance of *Pyramus and Thisbe*. Everyone enjoyed the Bergomask dance. The blessing of the house and the new marriages by the **fairies** represented an inner harmony, bringing peace, rest and good fortune.

As actors or members of the audience *The Dream* offers us choices about how far we uncover the deep motives of our lives and how far we can be hopeful and positive. Exploring those choices is an adult activity. *A Midsummer Night's Dream* is definitely not just for children!

INDEX